Made in the USA
Middletown, DE
25 May 2021

40377874R00073